also by eugene s. robinson:

Fight: Everything You Ever Wanted to Know About Ass-Kicking But Were Afraid You'd Get Your Ass Kicked for Asking [Harper Collins]
A Long Slow Screw [Robotic Boot]
Paternostra [Editions Inculte]
Les Sons Inimitables De L'amour [cipM]
Baretta [Ecrivains en Series, saison 2, Leo Scheer]

Eugene S. Robinson
p.o. box 19271/stanford/ca/94309
650/714/4891
ox_bow@hotmail.com
eugenesrobinson.com
facebook.com/eugenerobinson

Southern Records/Studios
10 Myddleton Road
London N22 8NS
tel +44 (0)208 888 8949
url www.southern.com

Copyright 2013
ISBN: 978-0-9566746-2-3
Catalogue number: 28174

Artwork & design by Jamie Lawson at Poly Studio
polystudio.ca · jamielawsonart.com

Back cover photo by Ulf Andersen
ulfandersen.photoshelter.com

THE
INIMITABLE
SOUNDS
OF LOVE

*A Threesome
in Four Acts*

eugene s. robinson

FEATURING:

ESTHER: *the 32-year-old wife of…*
SAM: *the professor and erstwhile neighbor of …*
HENRY: *the handsome*

ACT ONE

[The lovers loll in bed in various states of languid semi-dressed repose. It is late afternoon, though the room itself is sunless and windowless. The décor is mid-century modern more as an ironic tribute than an unstudied design choice. There is music playing. It is a gentle piano meander reminiscent of Bill Evans. If some would say it was the song The Nearness of You, they wouldn't be wrong.]

ESTHER: Did you ever think that in all of the beds all over…I mean anywhere there are beds with lovers laying in them…that though what happened may be exactly the same that everyone involved is convinced that they are totally different…

HENRY: No…

ESTHER: No, I mean not that they themselves are different. Well maybe I do mean that, but that circumstance is different. If you threw yourself off of a cliff and hit the ground and were only injured, instead of killed, and turned to someone laying next to you on the ground who had done the same thing do you think in your heart of hearts you'd persist in the belief that these experiences were not at all similar?

HENRY: You know an ex- once asked me what the difference was between me and a scumbag.

ESTHER: Hahahah…

02

HENRY: Well, yeah…I mean I think it WAS meant as a shot. But I took it seriously and somehow knew that of all the questions she had asked or would ask that my ability to answer this one was crucial if not to her and me, well definitely to me…

ESTHER: And what did you say?

HENRY: I laughed and then got very serious and said that the difference between me and a scumbag was that a scumbag invests almost 100 percent of their energy, well, energy that is not directed toward being a scumbag, in trying to convince other people that they are not scumbags. This is the thing…

ESTHER: Wait, so you're not a scumbag because you don't deny being a scumbag?

HENRY: Scumbaggery succeeds to the degree that it can exist in denial. Like that old saying about Satan and his most prominent victory being having convinced us that he doesn't exist.

ESTHER: Mmmm…I've always hated that. You know, the hustle: "I'm not being aggressive!" All while being aggressive. It's the liars and hypocrites that I hate.

HENRY: The systematic denial of the reality of experience.

ESTHER: You're a clever boy.

HENRY: I am.

ESTHER: But not so clever. I mean you actually didn't actually answer the question, did you?

HENRY: Hahaha…You're right I didn't.

ESTHER: Making you a scumbag?

HENRY: Making you impatient.

ESTHER: And if not a liar than a deceiver. But OK. I'm waiting.

HENRY: I'm not a scumbag because I own the ways in which I am a scumbag. I take full responsibility for the scumbag that I am. And I don't believe that anyone believes the opposite when I say I am a scumbag.

ESTHER: Oooo…you're very clever. Because those who are smart who, you have to admit, make much better prey, would assume that you were being modest and weren't half as much of a scumbag as you said you were. So not a lie for sure, but deceit.

HENRY: But realists would know otherwise. See the thing is…deceit preys on ignorance. *[waving his hands in the air with mock grandiloquence]* Where lies try to make idiots of us all and …

ESTHER: I think…

HENRY: Lemme finish *[more seriously now]*… I think if you listen long enough? Carefully enough… everyone will tell you everything they need you to know about them.

ESTHER: You're clever and bad. Because no one can possibly listen long enough and carefully enough when the inducements to not do so are so sweet.

HENRY: Is that the devil's fault?

ESTHER: I don't know that fault has very much to do with it at all. Sam will be home soon.

[There is a sigh and the lovers begin rising with a briskness, straightening bedsheets, dressing, opening the door to air out the room. Esther puts a pot on the stove, turns the flames up under it. And then to business.]

ESTHER: OK. Well, nice of you to come by…

HENRY: HAH…

ESTHER: *[archly]*…well it was. You know he almost found my diary the other day.

HENRY: What?

ESTHER: Yeah. I went to make breakfast and left it out. He came and handed it to me and said, "you left this out."

HENRY: Did he read it?

ESTHER: Based on the fact that he was still smiling when he handed it to me I would have to say no.

HENRY: You left it out.

ESTHER: *[gathering cups and tea bags from the cupboards]*…yes. Is that strange?

HENRY: Where did you leave it out?

ESTHER: On the bedside table. I was writing in it
            before I went to bed.

HENRY: And you left it out.

ESTHER: Hahaha…yeeeesssss….

HENRY: On his face?

ESTHER: I didn't leave it out on purpose if that's what
            you're getting at.

HENRY: Well, you know there's that weird human
            need to confess. Plays itself out all over the
            place.

06

ESTHER: Give me a little credit.

HENRY: I give you a lot of credit.

ESTHER: Besides which I never use your name. Just
            initials.

HENRY: I, myself, have never kept a diary.

ESTHER: Mae West said that every woman should
            keep one. She said keep one and one day it
            may keep you.

HENRY: How'd that work out for Mae?

ESTHER: She died falling out of bed.

HENRY: Diaries always seemed to me to be time bombs. The whens and wheres and how many dead later on were just, like, the smallest of the details really. I mean I remember once this woman I was fucking around with. She had got it in her mind that what she really wanted was to watch us having sex.

ESTHER: Mirrors?

HENRY: Well mirrors were where I first noticed it. At first I thought she was doing the vain woman thing: do I look okay? You know... something guys never think about when they are fucking since by virtue of the fact that we ARE fucking we've got as much of the Adonis thing going on as we need. Even if we're 35 pounds overweight and doing it in our parent's basements. Anyways, she'd do this thing where'd she'd say, "I had this fantasy..." And from there you could fill in the blank as to what the fantasy was and then I would typically say, "well, we should try it." You know so much of this was like being a shrink. Or a priest. Providing license where none other would.

07

ESTHER: Priest Henry. Wayward Priest Henry. Though calling you a wayward priest makes me think of altar boys.

HENRY: The fact that the church hasn't been ransacked for that fact alone is mind-boggling. So she says to me one day that she wants to watch us. I know what she is trying to say but I want to make her say it. So I suggest mirrors. And she mentions "or filming." Which is where I figured she was going the whole time with this. And so we did. But as usual when you open the gates to place where there are no gates all kinds of stuff comes flooding through. Right? From? Who the fuck knows? And I don't judge. Well, I guess I do, but nothing that came flooding through was making me judge. You know, it was suburban stuff. Filmed having sex in public. Filmed having sex in a CAR in public. You know....modern home videos. And then she hits on the idea of a group thing, which was something, she justified to herself that her husband would never do therefore giving herself license to do it without him. Did I mention she was married?

ESTHER: Haha....as well as I know you I had already guessed this. Did they have money too?

HENRY: Had you already guessed that too? Hah…
you guessed right then. So it was set up: she
and I would have sex, with another guy in
the picture and another guy filming said
picture. Perfect.

ESTHER: So you had sex with a man?

HENRY: Nooooo…

ESTHER: Yes, you did. You had sex with a man.

HENRY: Well in a manner of speaking I had sex
WHILE he was having sex, which is very
different from what you're suggesting,
haha…

ESTHER: Hey…I'm just calling it like you're saying it.

09

HENRY: The sexual activity that was occurring was
not explicitly or implicitly homosexual to
put a finer point on it. He stayed on one
end, I stayed on the other.

ESTHER: Does that make you feel better? Haha…
you were one bathroom break away from
complete and total man on man action.

HENRY: You're just funning me.

ESTHER: I'm just funning you.

HENRY: So, she's deep deep DEEP into this. The poor guy running the camera was dying, so we let him in too…

ESTHER: Wait. What's the attraction anyway? I mean you were already having sex with her, how'd it help for you to have help? I mean did you need the help?

HENRY: You forget it was her fantasy.

ESTHER: If her fantasy had been eating dog shit would you have helped with that?

HENRY: Well most of us have plenty of that to eat. But no. I'd have excused myself from that exercise and so yeah, OK. I was all in, as well. Which from your tone I guess would mean it's not one you've been all in on yourself?

ESTHER: Is that what I said? Or were you just fishing?

HENRY: The worst day fishing is better than the best day working, haha…and being in a group scene? It's like watching a movie, while being in a movie. Most guys like the media driven idea of them with two women. They only like that because they've never TRIED that. It's miserable. Unless it is driven by the women, in which case as the man you're just an afterthought anyway, it will be fraught

10

with peril. If one girl is too much better looking than the other? And you pay a little too much attention to the pretty one? You're sunk. If they don't like each other for any other reason? You're sunk. And then what one might do alone she's now suddenly shy about doing with another woman there. Watching. Judging. And then there's worse stuff, competing for intensity of orgasm, and suddenly as the man you feel like you're in deep water that's way too rough and you're actually not having fun at all.

ESTHER: This sounds a tad too personal for you.

HENRY: It was. Two fucking sisters at that. The worst of all possible worlds because in the end I really had only one cock, they were not going to commit incest so it was just a roomful of people waiting on ME. And let me tell you. No cock needs that kind of pressure.

ESTHER: hahah…

HENRY: Whereas when it is a woman and two men? It's like being in a movie and WATCHING a movie. It's great. And as long as that guy is not trying to do a sneak around the rear or one of those guys who likes to talk too much or high five you in the midst of fucking, well you're really going to be OK.

11

ESTHER: OK.

HENRY: So we're going at it, and it's working fine. Wonderfully. We finish up. And she asks for a copy. And as we pass over the copy I know that it could be six days, or six hours, or 17 months, but as my hand lets go of it and her hand takes it I know as sure as I am standing in that room, my shrinking cock bearing testament to what just happened, that her husband will find it and find out what just happened.

ESTHER: How do you know this?

HENRY: Like Mirbeau said, or to paraphrase, there are some backs that cry out for the knife, and this video cried out to be found because, you see, she would "leave it out."

ESTHER: Ohhhhh ho ho….long walk around the block for that one Mr. Henry. Well played. But my diary is in code. Did you all wear costumes and masks in your video?

HENRY: Noooooo….

ESTHER: So, did he find it? *[Esther, who has been making tea this whole time, pours them cups and they move off to the living room with saucered cups aloft.]*

HENRY: He sure did. About six months later. She
called me. We were done at that point
but being civilized people we maintained
a somewhat friendly fucking connection.
Emphasis on whichever one of those words
suits you. And she called and she was
hemming and hawing about some shit and
I was busy and just wasn't getting what she
was getting at and she finally blurted out,
"Jeff found the videos." And I could feel a
cold chill go up my spin.

ESTHER: Fear of the wrath of the vengeful husband?

HENRY: No. I never worry about this.

ESTHER: What? Why? I mean there's an entire
Western canon built up on the destruction
wreaked by men in love. Or is this some sort
of macho thing?

HENRY: Macho? No. Most guys initially are
convinced I'd be doing it to steal something
from them. If ever given a chance to explain,
and I never am, it's more like the scorpion
that stings to death the horse that's saved
him by swimming across the flooding river
with him on his back: it's what we do.

ESTHER: Wait, what? Destiny and form leading function?

13

HENRY: No. More "there but for the grace of god go I"....Of course, in this instance, "I" would be in a fine place. I mean I'm not a jealous man.

ESTHER: Says the egomaniac.

HENRY: Yeah, there are certain benefits to not realizing that you actually share the planet with anyone else. Anyway, he found the videos. She had "hidden" them in a place that would be impossible for him to find, in her closet, and find them he did.

ESTHER: Oh god.

HENRY: Well he found them and he watched them. I mean in this instance it's much easier to read a diary. You just look at the words. But he had to walk around the house and find something to play it on. And he watched.

ESTHER: What did she do?

HENRY: What would you have done?

ESTHER: That all depends.

HENRY: On?

ESTHER: Who the husband is?

HENRY: Who is your husband?

14

ESTHER: Sam. But we're not talking about me.

HENRY: I was asking you though.

ESTHER: Sam with a video would be like Sam with a diary. He wouldn't look.

HENRY: Well the question would be what would you do if he had looked?

ESTHER: You know, at that point I don't really think the next move is mine. I mean a picture is worth 1000 words and pictures like that probably have a much steeper exchange rate than that. But what did SHE do?

HENRY: She went straight to woman and started crying. And then straight to rote: he didn't understand her, he made her feel unattractive, she suspected he was having affairs...a veritable laundry list of exculpatory reasons why she was having sex with three men on video.

ESTHER: I wonder how much of it he watched. I mean I imagine you'd have watched the whole thing.

HENRY: I'd have watched it, and taken it and said nothing about it. Just for fun. And given a copy to my lawyer. Just in case. But the weird thing is we know he didn't watch the whole thing because he kept talking about the two guys she was having sex with. If he had watched the whole thing he'd have known that it was three guys that she had sex with at once.

ESTHER: And the upshot?

HENRY: He said, "well at least I have a wife who likes the spirit of adventure." Then she asked him if he wanted something to eat. He said "no" at first but then seemed to feel bad that he was denying her a chance to do something nice for him, so then he said "yes." And she cooked him some eggs.

ESTHER: And that was it?

HENRY: Well, she was so proud of him for being such a flexible and understanding modern man that she decided to never to do this again. That is: have sex with three men at once in their house. So as a sign of respect for him she'd only have sex with men in their garage.

ESTHER: Respect?

HENRY: Respect.

ESTHER: Oh. Sounds like Sam's here.

ACT TWO

[Sam enters. Bundling a large plastic basket full of laundry, bed clothes, underwear, and a box of soap powder balanced precariously on top, he shoulders through the door of the apartment, which he's kicked open with his legs. Not physically dissimilar to the darker Henry, he eyes them, first Esther and then with a brief nod to Henry, who is smiling widely.]

HENRY: Hahaha….last thing you want to see when you come home right?

SAM: Hi Henry.

ESTHER: What? *[She looks at Henry.]*

HENRY: Hahaha....he had a look. Like, well...I'm OK with the fact that I might be the last thing returning warriors want to see when they step in their houses.

SAM: Hahaha...nooooo...I'm always glad to see you Henry, you know that. *[Searching around for a place to put the laundry he eventually opts for the floor and crosses the room to where Henry is, sticking out a hand for a hearty handshake.]*

HENRY: Nice to see you too Sam.

ESTHER: *[smiling genially]* Henry just dropped by. He was giving me a backrub. His hands are so strong. I guess from giving backrubs. You should have him give you one too. Carrying all of that laundry upstairs.

SAM: Oh yeah?

ESTHER: Yeah.

HENRY: *[displeased with the prospect]* I actually was going to go and...

ESTHER: Nonsense. I mean he probably won't give you one as thoroughly as he gave me since he's pressed for time and all...

18

[They both watch Sam pull his shirt off and jump face down on the living room couch. Henry wants to touch him like he'd want to touch someone with the plague but is simultaneously so amused that he can't even look at the similarly amused Esther as they teeter on the edge of a laughter that would be called nothing but hysterical were they to give voice to it.]

SAM: I've been needing a good back rub. *[Henry touches the shirtless Sam tentatively.]*

ESTHER: You're going to make me out a liar now Henry…

SAM: Hmmm….

HENRY: What?

ESTHER: I tell Sam what strong hands you have and you're touching him like you're afraid you're going to bruise the fruit. *[laughs]* I swear to god, what are you thinking? If I go to the toilet you're suddenly gay?

SAM: Here we go again…

HENRY: Again?

ESTHER: Again. You men are so fueled on this fraternity fantasy of two women together that you never stop to consider, to flip things around so that it makes sense to you when someone is suddenly…

SAM: Yes dear.

ESTHER: Yes dear... *[slightly irked]* when Henry was giving me a back rub he was telling me stories about threesomes that he's had before and...

SAM: Ow, Henry. Your hands ARE kind of strong there. Easy big fella.

HENRY: Sorry.

SAM: *[with cocked eyebrow and head now raised off of the couch]* Threesomes? You mean like tennis doubles but without the fourth? A trio? Hmmm...

20

HENRY: Um...

ESTHER: Sure sure...a MENAGE.

HENRY: Well, I...

SAM: Honey, can't you see you're making our guest uncomfortable. Now Henry...

ESTHER: How could you make a man who has sex in PUBLIC uncomfortable? *[laughs]*

HENRY: Big difference between someone's house and a parking garage and... *[Henry sputters]*

SAM: Henry. This all stems from an incident my wife Esther has not quite talked out yet.

ESTHER: And Sam is quite the talker. So he'd know this for sure.

SAM: You see we had a threesome experience that did not go so well. Or as planned. Or as intended. Or desired.

HENRY: *[looking over the back of the prone Sam whose head is turned as he watches them while rising to sitting]* Well, this IS a surprise.

SAM: Is it? Hmm…Well I will tell you what's not a surprise. What's not a surprise, and not to be too terribly professorial about this but lack of thought is as damning to this field of play as it is to any battlefield. Witness: Custer's Last Stand. Classic underestimate of all of what was involved. As was my sense of propriety during an evening of drinks and socializing at a conference retreat when I asked a friend of Esther's to stay a bit longer after the company had gone.

HENRY: Stay?

SAM: Yes. Stay. She needed a ride to get to where she was going and we all had had so much to drink that we thought some coffee or at least some table talk would make the prospect of

21

driving her home without driving her home
drunk a little more sensible. And barring that
there was, well all of the private lodges had
guest rooms. So the guest room.

ESTHER: The guest room.

SAM: So after cleaning the dishes and dinner, and
the coffee, we decided to take a hot tub and…

HENRY: A hot tub?

ESTHER: WE?

SAM: Yes. We.

ESTHER: You asked me if I minded if she hot tubbed
with us.

SAM: *[patiently]* It was implied where this might
have been going.

ESTHER: Carrying an umbrella might imply a belief
in the possibility of rain, but could just as
easily be a way to protect you from the sun.

SAM: Esther…?

ESTHER: Don't get me wrong Henry. I am no prude.
And I was not blind to the implication.
As he was naked when he asked. But that
doesn't mean it was talked or thought out.

22

SAM: Agreed. In any case while we may differ now on which way we fell down the stairs, we still fell down the stairs. And so it was decided: a quick hot tub and then home with her. So we're in the hot tub…

HENRY: Who got in first? *[Henry moves off from near the couch to an easy chair]*

ESTHER: Why?

HENRY: The driver always gets in first right?

SAM: In fact he's right. Or at least from the viewpoint of whether we started out with clothes or not. I mean in America everyone does this with swimsuits on even though it's clear there'll be no swimming. In Europe? Without. In any case I started out in the house without. And lead Esther out to the tub. So she went without and our friend…

HENRY: Whose name was?

SAM: You don't know her.

HENRY: You're just going to call her "her" for the rest of the story?

SAM: Call her Eve then. She sort of stands there outside the tub, swaying a little bit from the drink and Esther and I start to kiss and we

23

wave her in. She shrugs, starts taking off her clothes and gets in. At this point no one's done anything that would make his or her mother cry, right? *[laughs]*. So Eve is sitting on the other side of the tub and Esther calls her over and…

HENRY: Wait. Esther calls her over?

ESTHER: So what? It was a friendly gesture.

HENRY: I am a big fan of friendly gestures. Made by naked women. In hot tubs. And I typically don't grouse about them after having made them.

ESTHER: The grouse is not where I am coming from on this though now if….

SAM: ANNNNDDDD….she climbs in next to Esther and everything is friendly.

HENRY: Good. We're back to friendly. I like friendly.

SAM: And I start rubbing their shoulders, a little light backrub…kind of like the ones you're fond of. They start kissing. And they are beautiful to watch. But you know I am not a big fan of porno. Unless it's got ME in it. And the kind of porno I LEAST like is girl-on-girl porno since it seems to me at that point you have TWO people faking it versus just the usual ONE. So they are kissing and I guess feeling some obligation to not leave me out of it, though I was content to just watch, Esther pulls me around to face Eve, and presumably to join in. And join in I do…

ESTHER: Join in is what you do at a dinner party when you sort of glide from one conversation to the next. Which you do with great regularity with greater deftness than you did this.

SAM: And we're almost to the rub, you see, what she's talking about is the penis. A corollary for the very real face of what it was we were doing. What HAD been happening was Harlequin romance-y…right up until you introduce the party guest that changes the party. The impudent cock. And there he is and there Eve was and what had been poorly thought out was now being acted out and well…

ESTHER: You did what men always do: imprint the situation with your desire.

SAM: But desire is what we were talking about.

ESTHER: Yes, COLLECTIVE desire, not your SPECIFIC desire and…

25

SAM: There is no collective without the individual aspect of...*[their voices are getting louder]*

ESTHER: The collective wasn't requesting your penis as an hors d'oeuvre!

SAM: Given that it was on the tray of hors d'oeuvres you can't have been blind to...

HENRY: WAIT! *[His shouting surprises what seems to be a semi-amusing routine that has been well-played, but unresolved, between them]* So, wait, what the hell happened after the dish was served or whatever the hell you all are talking about?

SAM: She started crying.

ESTHER: He started crying.

SAM & ESTHER: Eve started crying.

HENRY: Everybody was crying. Like at Bambi.

ESTHER: I don't know why I started crying. And to not be a complete child about this, yes, I started crying first, but it had nothing to do with jealousy. I mean I know Eve well enough to know that I would not lose him to her.

HENRY: Why would you care? *[They both look at him with different types of shock registering on their faces. Sam's is mock shock. Esther's is disbelief shock.]* I mean, I mean…that came out bad. What I mean is you can't have been thinking that in the moment right?

ESTHER: No. Not really. But I have to figure it was a calculation I was making. I mean that's part of jealousy right? It was not any of that typical feminine stuff. She didn't look better, was not sexier, or younger or had a better body or any of that.

HENRY: It was?

ESTHER: Being in the presence of, I guess, violent emotion.

27

HENRY: Which? Whose?

SAM: Passion is a violent emotion.

HENRY: Is passion an emotion?

SAM: Well it could be a philosophy but here, in this instance? Well, yes, we were FEELING passion as surely as Esther was feeling angry.

ESTHER: I wasn't angry. I was upset.

SAM: Upset then.

HENRY:	So what happened?
ESTHER:	What usually happens when everybody in the room starts crying?
HENRY:	The party stops?
ESTHER:	The party stops.
HENRY:	And the party stopped?
SAM:	Sure. All but the logistics. Did Eve get to stay? Or did she have to go? And if she went who drove her? If I drove her it would be uncomfortable if I was even a minute late. I mean who likes their coitus interrupted? So anything I did after that would have been understandable. I mean from the context of it all. And, of course, if she stayed, well, where would she sleep?
HENRY:	So…?
SAM:	Esther drove her home.
HENRY:	And when Esther was late? *[laughs]*
SAM:	I was asleep when she got back so I had no idea how late she was.
ESTHER:	Henry might remember that night too.

SAM: Really? How so?

ESTHER: I had to run back here after dropping Eve off to pick up some stuff and I ran into him. Literally.

SAM: Eh?

HENRY: *[a bit too quickly]* So lessons learned? Moral of the story?

SAM: Well that's where we had reached an impasse. I mean we were both turned on by it, but Esther felt like my failure to understand her breakdown as anything other than a sort of feminine over-reaction had meant that we'd never reach an understanding that would reestablish parity.

29

ESTHER: Pretty fucking simply Henry, if he didn't know how I felt it would always feel weird and be this sort of mark against me since it was me who acted out.

SAM: You want a drink Henry?

HENRY: No.

SAM: Of course not. You have to go. How selfish of us to be keeping you.

HENRY: Well, no. I mean, ok, a quick one.

SAM: A quick one. Esther?

ESTHER: A quick one will be fine by me too.

ACT THREE

[Sam starts to mix up some wildly complicated drinks. Crushed ice, mint, shakers, swizzle sticks, dashes of lemon and lime, salt, tasting, drinking, tasting again, and eventually a lit match and a sudden burst of upward shooting fire. Esther, still wearing the same dress shirt, oversized and belonging to Sam, coos excitedly, while Henry's mood visibly darkens along with what appears to be the day as night approaches, though there is no general sense of this without windows, a change of lighting signals the shift.]

HENRY: So what is this quick drink you're fixing me?

SAM: Us.

HENRY: Yes, us. What is it?

SAM: It's a little specialty of the house. I call it The Serum of Truth. *[laughs]*

ESTHER: Ooooo....what happens if someone who is perpetually truthful drinks The Serum of Truth?

SAM: I don't know. Anyone who is that, I mean.

ESTHER: You're married to one, dear. And don't you dare laugh. I've never told a lie my entire life.

SAM: Which is probably not even your first lie today.

32

ESTHER: You know in some places in town a man could get his ass kicked for talking like that.

SAM: Yes. To another man. Women work on a different kind of clock here, it seems. One that measures not the factual accuracy of any given statement or state of affairs… not the LITERAL accuracy of something or other. So you never hear a woman calling in to question another's truthfulness because veracity is only useful to them when talking to men. Or about them.

ESTHER: So all women are born liars?

SAM: I don't know anything about women, much
             less all women. But it seems to me that all
             women realize that the truth is complex
             and not to be delivered like some sort of
             happy greeting card at all. How many times,
             Henry, have you had a woman say to you,
             "Oh, come on, just tell me the truth?"

HENRY: I don't know.

SAM: But you HAVE heard it, right? And of the
             times you've heard it, spoken to you or
             someone else, how many times has the poor,
             hapless fellow it's been spoken to taken the
             bait and thinking it would quell the storm
             and quiet the inquiry, answered with what
             he considered the "truth" to be?

33

HENRY: I don't know.

SAM: *[looks probingly at Henry]* The answer is
             unimportant Henry because you know it's
             happened more than once and that's all that
             matters since on speaking the "truth" the man
             is dragged out, hung by his heels and beaten
             with chairs in the village square of feminine
             intrigue where the real objective is not the
             truth at all but the subjugation of the subject
             at hand: you. Or someone like you.

ESTHER: So why bother with the truth serum at all then? *[She reaches her hand up to receive one of the drinks that Sam is passing around now as he moves across the room.]*

SAM: It's like Ritalin. Did you know Henry that if you give Ritalin to a person who is NOT hyperactive it has a strangely opposite action on them, making them feel speedy, awake. Whereas if you give it to someone who is supposedly hyperactive, it calms them down?

ESTHER: So if you give truth serum to a pathological liar you…

SAM: I don't know Esther. And pathological seems a pretty strong word to use when we can't even agree on what, if any, any particular version of reality best even suits what we're doing now. But I do know *[passing a drink to Henry and sipping some of his own]* that this is probably the best one of these I have ever had, though.

HENRY: *[looking at his doubtfully]* I remember once I was at this party and this friend of ours came running in, breathless. And upset. She's waving her hands and we ask her what's wrong and she says that another friend of ours, Sammy, had tried to rape her. She had fallen asleep in the front seat of a car parked

34

in front and he had attacked her. Which
evenly divided the camp into those who
thought that Sammy would not EVER do
such a thing and those that were believers.
I listened to both sides and finally said that
out of all of the things that she came here
tonight saying, why would she choose this
particular thing – "Sammy tried to rape
me" – if it hadn't been true? It made sense
and because it made sense we jumped in
the car, the alleged attempted rape vehicle,
and started to trawl some of his known
whereabouts. We finally found him walking
down on 3rd street and we pull the car up
and say that we want to talk to him. "Talk"
here being a word that was at pretty wide
fucking variance to what was really going
to happen. And so we said that a claim had
been lodged against him regarding a possible
rape attempt. He called bullshit on that and
that's when the beating started. We beat him
savagely, and well, and the one among the
three of us judges who had the most level
head interrupted the beating every now and
then to say "it will be worse for you if you
don't tell us the truth." And with each bit of
beating we lent some truth to this larger bit
of truth and the beatings got worse. Until
he stopped calling her a lying bitch and then
finally said, "Ok. Ok…I was leaning over
the front seat to get the cigarette lighter to
light my cigarette and my cock fell out…"

35

A THREESOME IN FOUR ACTS   ACT THREE

A statement that in the midst of a very
serious and well-delivered beating created a
sudden shock of merriment. I mean we had
all, outside of the screaming and bloodied
and bleeding victim, had cocks our whole
lives and never once had had the occasion to
claim that it had just, in a fully clothed state,
SLIPPED out. IN, yes? Maybe. But not out.

SAM: Comedy saved the day!

HENRY: It saved that minute. You see when you're in
the midst of something like that, speaking as
one who was in the midst of something like
that, the urge to continue is overwhelming
and while we smiled, it surely was not a sign
that anything good was going to happen.
And we beat him and beat him until like
a tree he started to bend to the ground
and then we stomped and we have most
assuredly would have stomped his brains all
over the pavement had it not been for the
Puerto Rican drug dealers in the building
above who with the weight of superior
armaments, guns, I believe, got us to stop.
[Henry takes a sip of his drink finally.]

ESTHER: So that was it?

HENRY: No. We left him there on the pavement. And
drove away in this great quiet afterward.

36

SAM: You felt guilty.

ESTHER: You felt guilty?

HENRY: We were guilty OF nothing and so didn't feel bad for anything. I mean when you turn off the light in a lit room and it's dark, what do you feel?

SAM: Nothing?

HENRY: No. Ultimately satisfied that the world is working the way you expected it to.

SAM: Henry? When you look at Esther, what do you see?

HENRY: Esther.

SAM: Look at her.

HENRY: I am looking at her.

SAM: You're watching her. LOOK at her. Look at the carefully unbuttoned buttons at the top where if you peek between them you can see the rise of her breasts. At her legs crossed under her as she twitches her feet.

HENRY: Uh hunh.

SAM: Nice right?

HENRY: Uh hunh.

SAM: It's her turn Henry.

HENRY: Turn?

SAM: We have no hot tub here, but you don't need that kind of romance do you?

HENRY: HAH.

SAM: *[laughs as well]* Comedy saves the day again. Or it would. If I was being comedic.

HENRY: Well…Esther?

SAM: Yes…Esther…?

ESTHER: I'm sorry. I wasn't listening. *[laughter. And then quiet.]* Interesting book balancing.

SAM: Maybe. If it does indeed balance the books.

HENRY: Hmm…So you think you're all OK with this?

SAM: Sure.

38

HENRY: You have thought this through? You have taken into full account the images that will be burned into your head that you will never be able to un-see? You think it's enough to have imagined this to know what it's like? And you think that thinking about it is as easy as doing it?

SAM: Less sure.

ESTHER: Less sure?

HENRY: Only one way to find out. *[Henry crosses the room to where Esther is sitting and kisses her violently]* So this is OK? *[And shooting his hands under her shirt as Esther writhes in the full blush of animal joy, noisily voicing her endorsement]* And THIS? *[And the kissing and groping slows into an earnest passion filled embrace. Less flash, much more full-bodied and real].* You see *[slowing but not stopping what he's doing]* it's not enough to just not have a problem with this. You have to actually want this.

SAM: *[gamefaced, nods, but much less sure now]* Sure.

HENRY: *[removing his own shirt now]* So come on then *[both he and Esther start to move off back toward the bedroom, still embracing].* Come on. *[between kisses].* Be a man. *[This last gibe gets Sam and he rushes to follow them into the bedroom, closing the door behind him.]*

39

[Henry and Esther fall on the bed that they had just hours before risen from and continue, slowly disrobing now. Sam, though shirtless and in the room, is less sure of himself and tentatively takes off his pants while watching and looking for an opening. Henry sees him and backs away from Esther to give Sam an open avenue. Sam lowers himself slowly to the bed and kisses his wife, slowly, and the air feels like it's being sucked out of the room. Henry circles them, taking his clothes and everyone else's clothes off of the bed, and starts to fold them, while watching closely, and now, academically.]

HENRY: You know it's great that you can actually do this, Sam. You never know what a man's made of when it comes to this kind of thing. I mean it's all the problems usually present for a man with the ADDED difficulty of having whatever failings he has amplified in front of another man. Let's face it: most guys don't do this kind of thing around any more than one person. And some guys might get started but then they come too quickly. And some guys get here in the clutch and they can't get it up. Can you imagine that? It's SHOW time and you just CANNOT get it up. You just no way, no how can get it up!!! No matter how HARD you try? Haha…and the more you try, the more…I'm sorry. I'm talking too much. Am I talking too much?

40

ESTHER: *[Esther is now laughing. And kicking her legs as Sam rolls to the side, unsmiling]* Haha... stop it and come on, Bunny...

SAM: *[sitting up]* Bunny?

ESTHER: What?

SAM: You called Henry, Bunny.

HENRY: Did she?

SAM: *[now starting to stand up off of the bed, slowly]* She suuuure did. So you're Bunny.

ESTHER: Sam...

SAM: Bunny.

41

ESTHER: You read my diary Sam.

SAM: It fell from where you had left it.

ESTHER: I left it on my bedside table Sam.

SAM: Is that what you told him?

ESTHER: I left it on my bedside table. I had been writing in it before I went to bed.

SAM:	You left it on my face. Or at least that's where I woke up to find it. I had rolled over on it. So you may have been writing in it before you went to bed, but I woke up with it under my face.
ESTHER:	Doesn't change the fact that you read it nonetheless.
SAM:	Doesn't change the fact that he is Bunny.
HENRY:	Why Bunny?
ESTHER:	Henry. Honey Bunny. Bunny. Made sense at the time.
HENRY:	Makes sense.
SAM:	You know in some countries I'd be perfectly within my rights to shoot you right now. In some countries I'd be able to shoot you both.
ESTHER:	For?!?!
SAM:	Um. Disaffiliation of affections. Deceit. Infidelity, um…
ESTHER:	No one lied to you. And as we all stand, half-naked in the same bedroom, where would your defense of infidelity even start?

42

SAM: After you both died? Anywhere I wanted it to. What you two don't understand is that this all changes things. It changes everything in every way. I have gone from someone who was giving a gift to someone who has had one stolen. I have gone from a willing participant to an unwitting one. I have been tricked in the worst of all possible ways by a woman I should have thought would not have tricked me and by a man who I didn't think was smart enough to have done so. And I am now in the untenable position of being checkmated into any possible scenarios none of which serves me, or my interests. This is a woe is me moment if there ever was one. And even if you leave now, she will not. Or rather whether she leaves or stays I am in the same hell.

43

HENRY: Let me get this straight: five minutes ago it was "her turn"? And now it's not? Now it's hell?

SAM: Seems like she's had her turn. Many turns Many more turns than any of those I'd need to have balanced here.

ESTHER: Wait, wait, wait…if you read my diary why didn't it matter to you until now? Before Henry was Bunny who slept with your wife he was OK being Henry who was going to sleep with your wife? I think this is your vanity and sometimes life is about having that vanity fucking affronted. Many times, many more times than you may have even believed you could stand. But only NOW do you understand this? I don't think there's any other way you COULD have understood it.

SAM: Fuck you.

HENRY: That's a great idea! *[and Henry is on Esther again and Esther surprised now, shrieks and then laughs]* There are only two ways to get to the Cross Sam. *[his kisses are now loud and theatrical and all over Esther's face]* You either walk to it. Or you get dragged there. And you know what Christ discovered when he finally got there? Abandonment, despair and eventually release and then an uplifting joy.

SAM: I'm not so much a religious man, Bunny.

HENRY: Call me Henry.

ESTHER: He means you should stop being such a drag. And come on and relax a bit. *[Sam looks down and scuffs his feet like a chastened boy as he walks back to the bed.]* Because tomorrow we may die.

SAM: I'm not a drag.

HENRY: He's not a drag.

ESTHER: I'm sorry for calling you a drag. And stop crying *[she wipes tears off of his face]*. It's hard to have sex when people are crying.

SAM: I'm not crying.

HENRY: He's not crying. *[Henry moves back across to the bed turning off the light as he goes.]*

ESTHER: Yes.

45

46

ACT FOUR

*[A toilet flushes off stage and Esther re-enters flouncing on
the bed between Henry and Sam. The lights are up now
and softly shine by the bedside beside which they murmur.]*

SAM: And we're balanced.

HENRY: And we're guilty of nothing and so don't feel
bad for anything. I mean when you turn off
the light in a lit room and it's dark, what do
you feel?

ESTHER: Balanced. *[And she leans over and kisses Sam,
this time with a good deal more passion.]*

*[the lights flicker, and the music, which has been on the
whole time is more present and noticeable than not and
more likely than not is again The Nearness of You.]*

END